Sitting Up Front

Jacqueline Jernegan

AuthorHouse™
1663 Liberty Drive
Bloomington, IN 47403
www.authorhouse.com
Phone: 1 (800) 839-8640

This book is printed on acid-free paper.

ISBN: 978-1-7283-5984-7 (sc)

Print information available on the last page.

Published by AuthorHouse 04/22/2020

author HOUSE®

To my husband, Jerry, who
loved to hear our stories.

I'm just a little teddy bear, pleasures, I don't lack
I love my life, I'll tell you why
I know I'm loved right back

My owner saw me in a shop,
she liked me right away
She picked me up and smiled at me
And took me home that day

I live in her car, seems funny, I know
But I sit right up front
Always ready to go

She has big dog and grandchildren quite small

So I sit and just wait

For what duties befall

These duties are varied, it
depends who we're driving
I've had some mishaps,
But I seem to be thriving

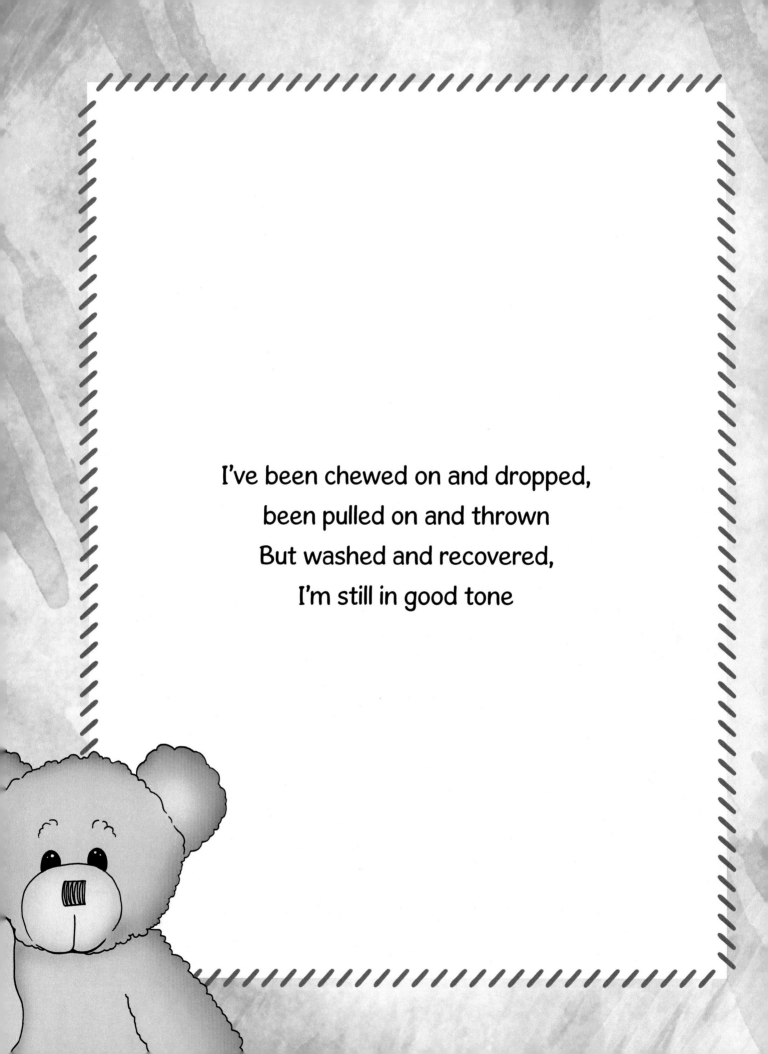

I've been chewed on and dropped,
been pulled on and thrown
But washed and recovered,
I'm still in good tone

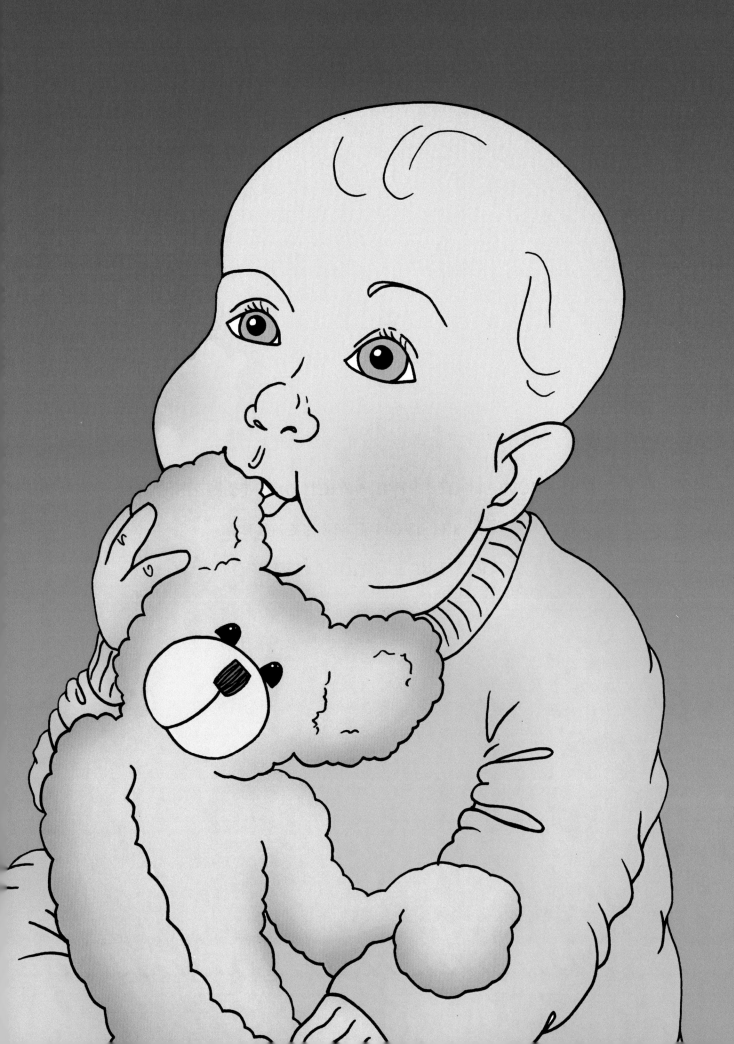

You know what I love, when one falls asleep,
I cushion their head
So their slumber is deep

The dog is quite nice, his excitement, well known
He sniffs me and sniffs me,
But leaves me alone

One day I was lost, a story worth tellin'

I was brought in the market

And left on a mellon

I guess someone knew I shouldn't be there
I don't look like fruit,
I'm a teddy bear

I was brought to an office and put on display
But my owner came back
To claim me that day

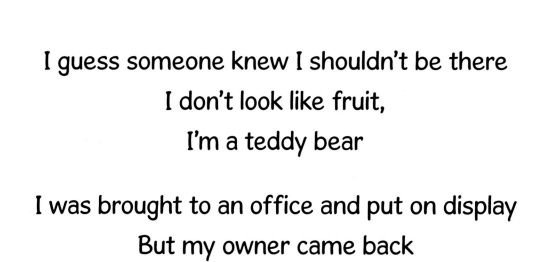

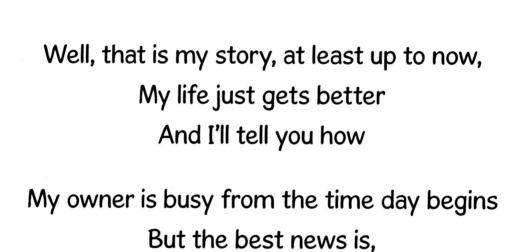

Well, that is my story, at least up to now,
My life just gets better
And I'll tell you how

My owner is busy from the time day begins
But the best news is,
We just had twins

Printed in the United States
By Bookmasters